Prophecy Made Possible
Yes You Can!

Dr. Linda K. Smith

Copyright © 2014 Free Them Ministries, Inc.

All rights reserved.

ISBN: 0966338456
ISBN-13: 978-0966338454

King James English used due to public domain.
We realize the KJV may be difficult to read and understand the vocabulary, however, you are encouraged to use any version of your choice.

DEDICATION

The hungry, curious Christians.

CONTENTS

INTRODUCTION	1
ARE YOU ALLOWED TO PROPHESY?	3
THE FIRST AND LAST PROPHETIC WORD	7
MANIFESTATION OR GIFT?	11
WHAT GOOD IS PROPHECY TODAY?	15
HOW DOES ONE PROPHESY?	19
WHAT HINDERS PROPHECY?	25
PRACTICE MAKES CONFIDENCE	29
HOLY SPIRIT AND YOUR LOCAL CHURCH	33
CONFIRMATION OR VAIN REPETITION?	37
THE NUTS AND BOLTS	41
CONTINUOUS PROCESS IMPROVEMENT	47

INTRODUCTION

They asked for it. Here it is. Following another conference where we demonstrated the prophetic anointing of God, people asked, "Do you have a book on prophecy?"

Because there are only about a million books already written on the subject of the prophetic ministry, none of which are as good as the Bible, I have avoided this task. I wasn't sure I had anything to add and didn't feel like I wanted to tackle the perfection or correction of previous information on prophecy.

However, God continues to give the people of God fresh insight into Holy Spirit's function so I suppose it's time to share. There are a lot of traditional thoughts on the manifestation of Holy Spirit. I hope to avoid the traditional all together, but I am still learning. Just when I am sure I fully understand, God opens a new realm of operation.

One of the joys of my ministry is seeing believers discover their supernatural life in Christ. That life is not reserved for some elite group of clergy. Holy Spirit serves every believer from day one of their faith.

In the footnotes for each chapter you will find a list of applicable scriptures. Some may be repeated. They bear repeating. Commit them to memory. They will sustain you as you manifest the power of God in a skeptical and harsh world.

Please notice that I try not to refer to Holy Spirit as 'the Holy Spirit', but rather use Holy Spirit as I would a name. We don't typically say 'the God' or 'the Jesus'. The name of this this 'person' of the Godhead is Holy Spirit. Also, I have attempted to omit gender language when referring to God and Holy Spirit. God is Spirit according to John 4:24 and Jesus said a spirit does not have flesh and bone. Gender is a flesh manifestation. Spirit is spiritual with no gender.

Are you ready to experience the fullness of God? Let's get started.

DR. LINDA K. SMITH

CHAPTER 1
ARE YOU ALLOWED TO PROPHESY?

Yes! You not only have God's permission and authority to prophesy, but the ability to do so came with 'the package', that is, with salvation. When you were born again, you actually were[1] sealed with Holy Spirit. It's in there. Traditionally we thought we had to tarry (wait a long time) and hope that God would slam us with speaking in tongues and then gift us with prophecy. This was often called a second in-filling or a latter work or the Baptism of the Holy Spirit.

You will continually run into the traditional line of thinking concerning operation of Holy Spirit. Traditional people can be violently adamant about their view point. Just remember that God is your heavenly Father and gives good gifts to the children of God and withholds no good thing from them.[2]

When Jesus breathed on the apostles and told them to receive the Holy Ghost (Holy Spirit)[3], the Greek word translated 'receive' is *Lambano* which means more than just receiving to yourself. It means others can readily tell you have received power from God. You are demonstrating the reality of being filled with Holy Spirit.

This is why, on the infamous day of Pentecost recorded in Acts, chapter 2 in the New Testament, we read about the dramatic

---

[1] Ephesians 1:13, 4:30
[2] Psalm 84:11
[3] John 20:22

demonstration of speaking in tongues. It left no doubt God had showed up in the form of Holy Spirit.

Just because Jesus told the apostles to go to Jerusalem and *wait* for the promise of the Father[4], traditionalists have thought we all had to wait, but apparently they didn't think we all had to do that waiting in Jerusalem. They had us on our knees at the front of the church for however long it took for us to finally do what God had empowered us to do the moment we got saved.[5]

Another popular blockade to manifesting Holy Spirit is to say it was just for the first apostles and ceased with them. However, in Ephesians, chapter 4, part of the gift ministry for the continuing edification and perfecting of the Church, are apostles and prophets. To buy into the idea that Holy Spirit manifestations stopped with the first apostles is to say Holy Spirit is not needed for the edifying and perfecting of the church and that God makes a difference between the Apostles who walked with Jesus and subsequent apostles. God is no respecter of persons (no partiality) so later apostles need what early apostles needed.

I will add here there are no restrictions for the operation of Holy Spirit. Both male and female may fully operate the power of God in all its manifestations. It also doesn't matter how long you have been born again. Day one, you can fully operate Holy Spirit for it is not by human power or might, but by the Spirit of the Lord.

It is the current theological understanding that only born-again people can operated Holy Spirit, therefore if someone seems to be flowing in a spiritual manifestation, but is not saved, it is false and from a demonic source. In general, I still believe that, however, never forget Balaam's ass.[6]

As believers, for us to operate fully in Holy Spirit, I do believe we must be saved. Think is, God is not limited or restricted and God can have rocks cry out or animals talk. God is Spirit and can operated as God sees fit.

Prior to salvation, I clearly heard the voice of the Lord one night, three times in a row and the instructions saved my life that night and I was saved later that month.

Paul, a later apostle, said he wished everyone spoke in tongues. He said he spoke in tongues more than all of them.[7] Was

---

[4] Acts 1:4
[5] Acts 11:14-17
[6] Numbers 22:21-38
[7] 1 Corinthians 14:5, 1 Corinthians 14:18

Paul out of line? Of course not! The book of Jude speaks of praying in the Holy Spirit (please stop calling it Holy Ghost!)

Jude says praying in (that is 'by') the Holy Spirit builds one up. Don't we still need to be built up? Yes.

Trinitarians who believe in all three presentations of the Godhead want to acknowledge Holy Spirit, but many want to limit what Holy Spirit may do. Apparently they think God is to be restricted from some of the more sensational activity God may desire. No more burning bushes, God! No more supernatural activity! God, you must act decently and in order according to our definition!

We can no more deny Holy Spirit free flow than we can stop Jesus from being Lord.

Although I was taught initially in ministry training that I could and should operate Holy Spirit, there were rules. One rule was that in an assembly, there had to be at least two people who spoke in tongues and that they each had to interpret their *own* tongues. This was strictly enforced.

We were told about denominations who taught that only the leader of the group (almost exclusively male) could interpret the tongues. We were taught this was legalistic, controlling and wrong according to scripture.

I had the opportunity as a children's pastor to attend a conference held by Willie George in Broken Arrow, Oklahoma. In one workshop, two people stood up and spoke in tongues, one at a time. My legalism was at full alert because the first person did not interpret after they spoke. Only thing is, I seemed to have the interpretation! If things were working as I had been instructed at the time, I should not have had the interpretation!

After the second person spoke in tongues, the male leader of the workshop interpreted. (I only mention the gender of the leader here because it played into my prejudice that 'religion' was sexist and operated Holy Spirit incorrectly.) His interpretation was exactly what I received in my Spirit. You can imagine my confusion.

God spoke to me, asking, "What's your problem?"

I answered, "Well Lord, you know they didn't do it the way I was taught scripture dictates."

To which the Lord asked another question, "Was it by the Holy Spirit?"

"Yes, Lord," I replied.

"Well, then, why do you have a problem? Can't I do it any way I want?"

"Yes, Lord." The Lord went on to point out that even when Holy Spirit may be handled incorrectly, God was well able to bring the correction, but in the way God wants to bring correction which may not match what I think should happen. Even handled incorrectly, it's still Holy Spirit.

I began to understand that the interpretation of scripture must come from scripture and not from humans. We tend to be too literal or too figurative in our own interpretation.

This was the beginning of being set free from boundaries of religion. Oh, make no mistake, we must still check everything with scripture . . . including our preconceived notions of theology.

I realize not everything done in the name of Holy Spirit is from Holy Spirit, but if the word of God does not expressly forbid or contradict the manifestation, it is wise to wait, ask God and learn from God.

Do you believe God can let you know in your Spirit if you are doing something wrong? Then do what scripture says and test God, try the spirits[8], go ahead and prophesy. God will confirm God's word even when it is in the form of your prophetic voice.

Although we must always use scripture as our basis for judging what is from God and what is from another source, we can err grievously in our judgment if we misinterpret scriptures through our own prejudices and misconceptions.

Recently, I was visiting with a pastor who told me of a woman who rejected the manifestation of gold dust appearing on some believers and that being attributed to God. The woman said she didn't see in the Bible where God had ever put gold dust on people therefore, she didn't think it was from God.

I pointed out that there was no scripture confirming it was ok for there to be a burning bush prior to Moses' experience with a burning bush and that even scripture acknowledges not everything that God did is written in scripture.[9]

No matter who tells you that you may not or cannot prophesy, I assure you, they are wrong. All you need is Holy Spirit and you are good to go. Let Holy Spirit flow.

---

[8] 1 John 4:1, Malachi 3:10
[9] John 21:25

CHAPTER 2
THE FIRST AND LAST PROPHETIC WORD

The first prophetic word was, of course, restoring creation to its original state. We could go back further, I suppose, and say it was when God created everything in the first place.

Yes, for those of you who like to argue scripture, I do believe in what you call the 'Gap Theory', but an adjusted form. I don't believe that creation and science always contradict one another. Man cannot discover anything in science without using what God created.

For those of you who have never heard of the Gap Theory, here it is in a tiny nutshell. God created everything perfect. Lucifer sinned and was thrown out of third heaven and subsequently trashed things on earth. In Genesis 1:2 the earth is without form and void, unlike something the way God would create it. In Genesis 1:3 and beyond is God speaking creation back into what can sustain the human race and brings glory to God. I don't buy everything mentioned in the Gap Theory, but I sift it through Holy Spirit.[1]

So in Genesis 1:1 we see a recorded account of God's creation and in Genesis 1:3 and continuing through chapter 2, we see God restoring. God did not *create* (Hebrew, *bara)* light in chapter one. God *said* let there be (Hebrew, *hayah)* light and there was light.

---

[1] Wikipedia contributors. "Gap creationism." *Wikipedia, The Free Encyclopedia,* 8 May. 2014. Web. 7 Jun. 2014.

God is light[2] according to scripture. God did not have to create light because God *is* light. God had to restore light upon the earth.

Considering John, chapter one, I believe the word spoken by God in Genesis 1 is a prophetic utterance proclaiming that Jesus, the Light of the World, would bring light to a darkened planet.[3]

The word of God is, simultaneously, type/figure/shadow, literal, and prophetic. It just depends on when someone reads it and the application of the reading. For example, the animal sacrifices at the tabernacle and temple found in the Old Testament literally happened. We can read the details for our learning, understanding what actually took place in that time.

They are also a type, figure and shadow. When we read of the scapegoat, we understand it is a type of Jesus who took our sins upon himself in a sacrifice. This, of course, makes the account also prophetic for those reading it prior to the crucifixion and resurrection of Jesus Christ.

When you study scripture, view it from these three aspects and you will gain revelation knowledge of God and God's Kingdom.

The last prophetic word can never be spoken for God is eternal. There is always a future in God. Paradise is not the end. There is no one time blanket prophetic word settling all of eternity. As long as God and God's children are speaking by Holy Spirit, there will be prophecy.

You have the privilege of joining in that utterance, now and forever.

The prophetic word from your mouth will live on until it is fulfilled or God alters it. Why would God alter a prophetic word? Read the story of Nineveh in the book of Jonah. Jonah gave a prophetic word against Nineveh and sat down on a hill to watch the judgment. The judgment never came because Nineveh repented.

You can also read the account of King Hezekiah[4] who received a prophetic word to get his house in order because he was going to die. However, the king prayed and the prophecy was delayed fifteen years.

Some people expect each prophetic word to happen in their lifetime in their sight, but God is not restricted by time. A prophecy

---

[2] 1 John 1:5
[3] John 1:9
[4] 2 Kings 20

may take decades to unfold even if it does happen in the lifetime of the prophet or recipient. Take the case of Abraham and Sarah in the book of Genesis. They received a prophetic word concerning having children, but did not see that come to pass through God's power until they were very old. At one point, they were so tired of waiting, they had children through a bondwoman which was not God's plan. When we give or receive a prophetic word, by faith, we trust God to carry it out in God's timing and God's way.

I remember as a young Christian hearing God speak to me. God said, "I'm going to give you a new husband, the husband you deserve."

Because I had been dissatisfied with the speed of Christian growth in my husband (I was a very young and new Christian, but thought I knew it all), I had been complaining to God about my husband. I thought this prophetic word meant a husband who was a different individual and I didn't even consider that would mean a divorce. We can be so silly sometimes, can't we? I also thought this would take place quickly.

It took a few years, but I did get that new husband the Lord promised. It was my husband as the New Man Christ made of him. We were married almost 39 years before he died and he had become a passionate lover of God, a pastor and the best husband I could have ever imagined.

CHAPTER 3
MANIFESTATION OR GIFT?

It is amazing to me that God will give Christians something and then man's doctrine tries to take it away from some or all of the intended receivers.

We need to get this truth in our hearts; God is no respecter of persons.[1,2] God is a God of equity. God loves us equally. The commandments, the promises, and the gifts all must be appropriated the same for everyone. Break the commandments, there are results. Keep the commandments, there are blessings.

One of the English words translated from Greek that has been used to rob God's people is found in 1 Corinthians 12. It is the Greek word, *pneumatikos*. For some strange reason it was translated into English as *spiritual gifts.*

In fact, the word 'gifts' in the first verse of 1 Corinthians 12 is not in the Greek language. In most King James version Bibles, *gifts* is in italics meaning the translators added it because, in their opinion, it aided translation. Most italicized words cause no problems. However, occasionally they can caused a change in understanding and therefore cause a wrong doctrine to evolve.

In the case of 'spiritual gifts' a wrong doctrine occurred. As humans we thought of how we give gifts and applied that to God's

---

[1] 2 Chronicles 19:7, Acts 10:34, Romans 2:11
[2] Hebrew, *masso'* paniym, partiality. Greek, *prosopolemptes*, one who discriminates.

giving of things. Take the word gifts out and use the meaning of *pneumatikos* and we have a perfected understanding. *Pneumatikos* means pertaining to the spirit. God did not want us to be ignorant of that which pertains to the Spirit.

What was wrong with the doctrine men applied to this passage? Men began to teach that God picks and chooses to whom and when God bestows a particular gift, in this case, one of the nine manifestations mentioned in the chapter. People were taught it was by works they could obtain one or two or more of the so called gifts. People began to think God was withholding from them and they had to earn these manifestations one by one.

However, the gift is Holy Spirit[3]. Salvation is a gift[4] of grace and faith.[5] When Jesus told the disciples to go to Jerusalem and wait for the promise of the Father which is power from on High, the result would take place *after* the resurrection. Why? Because then and only then could the disciples be saved and positioned to receive the Gift, that is the indwelling of Holy Spirit, or power from on high as scripture puts it.

To become saved, we confess with our mouth the Lord Jesus Christ and believe in our heart that God raised Him (past tense) from the dead.[6] The apostles definitely had already confessed Jesus as Lord, but until Jesus resurrected, they could not believe God raised Him from the dead. Once they could believe this, they received salvation and had access to Holy Spirit made available to them on the day of Pentecost as described in Acts 2.

Just because they had to wait, we do not have to wait any longer. What pertains to the Spirit is ours now. Later as recorded in the book of Acts, we can read of people immediately speaking in tongues upon salvation and there are some who did so after a period of time passed.

Let God out of the box. God can do things the way God wants, not the way theologians dictate.

There are other things translated 'gifts' in the English language of scripture. For example, the ministry is called gifts.[7] Prior to naming the functions and describing the work of the ministry in Ephesians 4, scripture translated into English says gifts were

---

[3] Acts 10:45

[4] Greek, *dorea*, gift

[5] Ephesians 2:8, also *dorea*

[6] Romans 10:9-10

[7] Ephesians 4:8

given unto men. The word 'men' is Greek, *anthropos* which can be male or female. The word 'gift' is Greek, *doma,* and means a gift, but the root word, *didomi* means to furnish what is necessary.

Therefore, God supplied what was necessary to all humans. It is not apostles; and some, prophets; and some, evangelists; and some, pastors and teachers who are the gift. It is what these functions provide that is the gift. I am a teacher. I did not receive a special gift and that makes me special. God wanted humans to be taught and I am one of many people who get the privilege to teach others. That function is part of what is necessary.

When a believer is obedient and available, they can function in one, two or all of these areas. Why we thought that a man vs a woman had to be especially singled out by God and gifted in one area his whole life is a mystery and not a God mystery.

So we see that the function of a Prophet is necessary and therefore, God supplies prophecy. We all can prophesy and there are those individuals who are tasked with functioning as a Prophet within the Body of Christ to humans.

Another Greek word that is translated as gift(s) is *charisma*. In 1 Corinthians 12 we see in English, the phrase, gifts of healing.[8] *Charisma* means, a favor with which one receives without any merit of his own. It is from another Greek word, *charizomai,* meaning to do something pleasant or agreeable (to one), to do a favor to, gratify. Healing from the Lord can legitimately be called a gift, but the gift is available to all through Holy Spirit by the stripes of Christ. Miracles bring healing, but are also by Holy Spirit. These are *pneumatikos* or things pertaining to Spirit.

In this book, we are specifically dealing with prophecy, but we should get the understanding that the operation of Holy Spirit whether it be the fruit of the Spirit[9], the manifestations listed in 1 Corinthians 12, or any other way God wants Holy Spirit to function does not happen because there is a special person whom God favors over others of God's children. YOU who are saved have Holy Spirit and CAN manifest thereby fulfilling God's purpose and glorifying God. Now THAT is special!

I was teaching a class on the very subject of being able to operate Holy Spirit in all its fullness when I noticed a woman crying. She had been raised in a denomination that didn't teach the members to operate Holy Spirit in manifestation. She had

---

[8] 1 Corinthians 12:9, 28, 30
[9] Galatians 5:22-23

been hungry for more of God and had found her way to a church outside that denomination and was then taught about Holy Spirit, but was, by their doctrine, restricted to just one of the nine manifestations listed in 1 Corinthians.

I asked her why she was crying. At first she couldn't speak because she was so overcome with emotion. I pressed on and she finally told me she was overwhelmed to realize she could have *all* of Holy Spirit and not just a part. She felt the freedom of the love of God that her heavenly Father gave her full access to Holy Spirit.

Don't allow man-made doctrine to rob you of your God-given gifts and abilities.

CHAPTER 4
WHAT GOOD IS PROPHECY TODAY?

The purpose of the prophetic utterance today is the same as it has always been. Again, let's look at the original language of scriptures. The first place we see the words prophet or prophecy or prophesy is found in Genesis 20:7 concerning Abraham. God spoke to Abimelech, king of Gerar, in a dream and called Abraham a prophet.

Now, of course, this is a time prior to the mass infilling of Holy Spirit to believers as seen in Acts 2, but remember that Abraham was a God man. He had favor as a God man. By the way, you have favor as a God person if you are born again. Don't you know that as a joint-heir with Christ, God really likes you?[1]

The word translated prophet in this passage is Hebrews, *nabiy'* *and* means spokesman. The root word is Hebrew, *naba,* to speak. Can you speak? Can the Holy Spirit in you hear God? Should God give you something to say, would you say it? Hmmm, then I guess you could prophesy!

Not until Paul began to write what God spoke, did we have a detailed description of the purpose of prophecy. Just by godly logic, we see that the purpose of prophecy is for God to speak to people through people, what God intends to happen. God just

---
[1] Romans 8:17

loves people.

God has spoken by a prophet to people who would not otherwise hear God. God has spoken through a prophet, corporate prophetic words to nations. God speaks to the Church through the prophetic voice. God has not stopped speaking and prophecy is still a necessary function of Holy Spirit.

The apostle Paul wrote so eloquently and thoroughly concerning the prophetic. In Corinthians, Paul told us prophetic utterances were to edify the Church.[2] (Again, sorry for the Old English Just read around it! It's easy. Just change words ending in *eth* to ending with *s*).

> 1 Corinthians 14:1-4
>
> Follow after charity, and desire spiritual gifts, but rather that ye may prophesy. For he that speaketh in an unknown tongue speaketh not unto men, but unto God: for no man understandeth him; howbeit in the spirit he speaketh mysteries. But he that prophesieth speaketh unto men to edification[3], and exhortation, and comfort. He that speaketh in an unknown tongue edifieth himself; but he that prophesieth edifieth the church.

Paul went on to further explain or rather compare tongues with interpretation to prophecy.

> 1 Corinthians 14:21-25
>
> In the law it is written, with men of other tongues and other lips will I speak unto this people; and yet for all that will they not hear me, saith the Lord. Wherefore tongues are for a sign, not to them that believe, but to them that believe not: but prophesying serveth not for them that believe not, but for them which believe. If therefore the whole church be come together

---

[2] 1 Corinthians 14:1-6
[3] Promoting another's growth in Christian wisdom, piety, happiness, holiness. Building up.

into one place, and all speak with tongues, and there come in those that are unlearned, or unbelievers, will they not say that ye are mad? But if all prophesy, and there come in one that believeth not, or one unlearned, he is convinced of all, he is judged of all: And thus are the secrets of his heart made manifest; and so falling down on his face he will worship God, and report that God is in you of a truth.

Paul was speaking to post-resurrection believers. The clock has not run out on this. Paul's words are as true today as they were when he received them from Holy Spirit.[4]

Does the Church still need edifying? Yes! If not, then we no longer need ministry, for part of the function of the ministry as seen in Ephesians, chapter 4, is for the perfecting of the saints, the edifying of the Body of Christ.[5]

We still need edifying, therefore we still need prophecy.

---

[4] 2 Peter 1:21
[5] Ephesians 4:12

CHAPTER 5
HOW DOES ONE PROPHESY?

Think of the moment you became a Christian. *How* did you do that? You simply believed what God said and did, you acted on it and you were saved. Prophesy has one pre-requisite. It comes through Holy Spirit. Born-again believers have Holy Spirit. Why?

The death, burial and resurrection of Jesus was a game changer. It began the New Covenant, a new way of doing things. At that point, God wasn't just limited to an occasional prophet like Elijah or Jeremiah. At that point, God had a vast and growing family of children through whom to speak. The new birth in Jesus Christ is the only way to appropriate the authority and ability to operate things pertaining to the Spirit of God.

That relationship being established, you now believe what God says and you speak. Speak what God says when God says to speak. Actually, I can take it a step further. Paul said in Corinthians that the spirits of the prophets is subject to the prophets.[1] Whoa!

The word translated 'subject to' is Greek, *hypotassō* and means to arrange under, to subordinate. The word spirits is plural because prophets is plural. In other words, the spirit in each prophet is subordinate to each prophet. Sure, I can choose *not* to prophesy, but I can also choose to prophesy. I choose to

---

[1] 1 Corinthians 14:32

consistently seek Father God in the realm of flowing with Holy Spirit.

As a Holy Spirit-filled, obedient vessel for God's purpose, I do not have to wait for a sign in order to prophesy. I don't need goose bumps, sweaty palms, shaking right hand, tears or any other fleshy occurrence in order to prophesy. I simply flow with God through my faith in God, open my mouth and say what God is telling me to say.

Jesus did what He saw the Father do and said what He heard the Father say.[2] He always did the will of His Father. So ought we to do. If God wants me to evangelize, teach, preach, prophesy, pastor, be apostolic, love, have joy, peace, gentleness, goodness, longsuffering, be meek, receive word of knowledge, word of wisdom, have faith, work miracles, discern spirits, heal the sick, etc., then that is what I choose to do.[3]

Don't limit God in what you will obey. Don't quench Holy Spirit.[4] Don't grieve Holy Spirit.[5] Be usable in any and all ways God desires.

I want to add here that God, being let out of our boxes, can prophesy through an unbeliever, but it would take a believer or believers to recognize those words as prophetic and distribute their meaning to others. For example, one prophetic person I know of often gets revelation and understanding through statements made by sports heroes or politicians. Then this believer communicates the understanding to the church.

Different people receive prophetic words in differing ways. It can be any or some of the following, but not limited to these:

- Dreams
- Visions (Closed or open eye)
- Smells
- Sounds
- Physical sensations
- Environmental changes
- Audible words
- Inaudible words
- A sign (something you encounter in the natural that

---

[2] John 8:28, 38
[3] 1 Corinthians 12:7-10, Galatians 5:22-23
[4] 1 Thessalonians 5:19
[5] Ephesians 4:30

quickens your spirit with a prophetic understanding)
- Just a 'knowing'

A few words of caution; don't copy someone else unless God is telling you to do the same thing. Don't think God will always inform you in the same way every time. Be open to whatever God is doing.

I remember a time when my husband and I were sitting in the outdoor dining section of a local restaurant. The weather was beautiful, my conversation with my husband was interesting, the food was good and there was the sound of traffic and the conversations of the other diners.

My spiritual attention began to be drawn to a couple of women at an adjoining table and one lady in particular. I didn't want to be bothered in that moment with information through Holy Spirit. As a pastor, I considered myself 'off the clock'. However, Holy Spirit was persistent and soon all the other sounds and activities took a back seat to this lady and what God was revealing.

My husband had learned that look I would get when this would happen and knew I wouldn't be much company for a few minutes. Finally I could resist no more and asked the Lord how and when to deliver what was being revealed to me. The other diners left and only the two ladies and my husband and I were remaining. Isn't God amazing to orchestrate it this way?

It was time for my husband and I to leave so I obediently walked past their table, stopped and said to the lady "I realize this is weird because you don't know me, and I don't know if you believe in such things, but the Lord has given me a message for you. . "

I told her what the Lord said, she cried and thanked me and I left her there to think about what the Lord had imparted.

Just be obedient in the moment.

I have seen people minister in a way their favorite minister did it one time and they fail miserably. Why? Because they aren't getting what the Father wants them to do. They are just mimicking someone else. The other person may have done exactly what God wanted them to do at the time, but that does not mean it should be done like that every time. Be like Jesus and do what God shows you to do.[6] Say what God tells you to say. Could just

---

[6] John 5:19

mimicking what others do without instruction from God fall under the category of vain repetition? Perhaps.

In my ministry, God has used all of the methods I listed. Sometimes God confirms the prophetic word through using multiple ways prior to delivery. Let me share more examples. Again, don't copy me. Get what and how God wants you to say or do when you prophesy or minister in any area.

One way I really enjoy receiving the prophetic word is through pictures that I draw. When I am going to speak at a meeting where I've never spoken before, God will begin to literally show me the room in which I will speak. God will show me individuals who will be there and tell me what to say to them. I have a background as an artist so I draw what God shows me marking where the individuals will be and making notations about what God said to tell them.

This can be very detailed down to where they will sit or be standing when it is time to minister to them. Still I have to be focused on Holy Spirit at the moment of ministry or I will mess things up.

At one meeting, God told me to minister to a girl with long beautiful red hair and told me what to tell her. At the meeting, I was impressed to have a woman there act as a go-between and she was to pick, by Holy Spirit who to bring up for ministry. She was so brave. I really, or rather God really put her on the spot. But she did what I asked and she brought up a woman. The woman she brought was tall and hand a scarf completely covering her head. She looked like she had been through quite a lot of tribulation.

As I looked at her, God brought to my Spirit, the girl with the long red hair. I could tell she either didn't have hair or didn't have much hair, but by obedient faith I asked her if she had long red hair (curly, by the way). She and a friend who was standing with her both made a sudden gasp. She started to cry. She told me she did indeed once have long curly red hair, but due to chemotherapy she had lost it all.

Holy Spirit then told me exactly what to say. I told her God saw her as a healthy young girl with beautiful long curly red hair. God wanted her to know God was restoring her health, beauty and vitality. She was blessed, God was glorified. I was obedient.

Another example would be when God gives me a list rather than pictures. I will get names, information on their emotional state, or life events. Before one meeting I saw a literal sign. It was like a long triangle laying on the long side and in the middle of the sign were the words 'my daughter' going toward the wide end as thought they were being screamed. I saw a woman with brown hair screaming 'my daughter'. I knew she had lost her daughter and was grieving horribly after the fact and that this was causing her to shut down her life. The Lord also gave me a name for the same meeting and I thought they were two separate ministry opportunities.

During the meeting, I found and ministered to the woman who had lost her daughter. It was powerful and she was set free from the overwhelming grief.

I the asked if there was someone there with the name I was given. No one answered. However, the husband of the lady who lost her daughter raised his hand. The name I mentioned was the name of their daughter! Their daughter had committed suicide and they couldn't understand why. With what the Lord showed me about the name of their daughter, they gained insight into her emotions leading to the suicide. It brought closure.

I can smell cancer. Now, listen, remember what I said. Don't just copy this. You don't have to smell cancer to minister healing and I don't always smell it. I smell it when it is a certain type and cause of cancer. I did not smell my own cancer nor my husband's cancer, but I have smelled cancer.

There are certain types of mental conditions that I can smell. I don't understand this, but there it is. Let Holy Spirit out of the box. God can reveal however God chooses.

CHAPTER 6
WHAT HINDERS PROPHECY?

Three great hindrances to anyone flowing in the prophetic are fear, doubt and pride. Time and time again I have seen the wheels come off as someone tries to prophesy because one or more of these three are present. I have seen individuals start out in the same meeting flowing strong in the prophetic and suddenly one of these rears its ugly head and, boom, the flow stops. They may keep talking, but you can watch as the crowd starts to realize the prophet is in his or her flesh and not in the Spirit of God.

I have to give some spiritual impressions I have about each of these. This is just my observation and understanding. Don't make a doctrine out of this.

Of course fear is a spirit[1] and I see it as an attack on the believer that requires a spiritual solution. Holy Spirit gives us the ability to discern spirits[2] and we can, by the name of Jesus, cast out evil spirits.[3] We can cast fear out of ourselves by the name of Jesus.

I know, I know. You thought another person has to cast them out of a person. We are not talking about possession by an evil spirit. We are talking about a Holy Spirit-filled believer being

---
[1] 2 Timothy 1:7
[2] 1 Corinthians 12:10
[3] Mark 16:17

oppressed by a spirit of fear. Tell it (fear), in the name of Jesus, to go and not return. For fear to stay, it has to be indulged as a house guest. It must be fed regular meals (our negative words), it must have a comfortable atmosphere (our negative thoughts), and it must be entertained (our negative actions or inaction caused by fear).

God has done all God can do to enable us to live free from fear.[4] If we want to prophesy accurately, bringing glory to God and blessing to God's people, we have to deal with that spirit of fear once and for all. The enemy will try to bring it back occasionally, but once you have the victory over fear, you simply re-enforce it. Remind yourself and the enemy that you have God's power, God's love and the sound mind of Christ.[5]

Doubt is a form of fear. It is proceeded by a poor thought process. Doubt is a lack of identity in Christ. Since God says we are more than conquerors in Christ Jesus,[6] doubt is believing the opposite of that truth.

When we allow doubt it is usually self-doubt. We doubt our ability to hear God and minister effectively. We assume the worse. However, do you realize that self-doubt is also doubting God? It is God who makes us able so if we doubt we are able, we are doubting that God made us able.[7]

Jesus once told the disciple not to think about what they would say in a difficult situation because the Holy Spirit would let them know what to say when it was time to speak.[8] If you are concerned about what you will prophesy, you are not trusting Holy Spirit. Relax and enjoy the power of God.

Moving on to pride, I personally hate this one. It is ugly. It steals the glory from God. When a person begins to operate in pride it's as though they are saying to God, "I've got this. I don't really need you. My skills are such that I can do this on my own."

Scripture says pride goes before a fall[9] and sure enough, the proud 'prophetic person' will soon fail in their attempt to flow with Holy Spirit. What makes me hate this one so much is the negative impact it has on the people God wanted to bless, heal and deliver.

---

[4] 2 Timothy 1:7
[5] 1 Corinthians 2:16, Philippians 2:5
[6] Romans 8:37
[7] Hebrews 1:7, Philippians 2:13
[8] Luke 12:11-12
[9] Proverbs 16:18

When I see pride on a minister, I must remind myself that pride is originally from Lucifer.[10] God hates the pride, but loves the person. Pride has a rebellious nature. There are approximately 46 places in the KJV English translated 'pride'. I suggest you look them up and study them. This will give you an understanding to deal with pride whether in yourself or others.

What can be done in a meeting if one or more of these three has caused a problem? If you are ministering alone (you are the only presenter), you need to recover as you go and begin a better flow. If you can't recover quickly, you probably need to end the meeting. It is better to stop than to do further damage.

If you are ministering in a team or have someone with oversight, hopefully they will be flowing better than you are at the moment and can bail you out, saving the meeting, glorifying God and blessing the people. As a pastor and leader, I have always tried to fix this in a way that does not embarrass anyone nor shame the ministry. If I walk in love, God gives me the methods to redeem the time.

The best way to avoid these three traps is to deal with them *before* you minister. Renew your mind daily.[11] Practice humility.[12] Winning athletes are those who have sharpened and maintained their fitness and skills before the test.

Prevention is not a dogmatic routine, i.e. speak in tongues 45 minutes a day, read through the Bible every year, pray through your list twice a day, never miss church attendance. Prevention means to consistently invest yourself in your relationship with God. Speak and listen to God throughout your day. Love on God. Spend quality time with God.

---

[10] Isaiah 14:12-17
[11] Romans 12:2
[12] 1 Peter 5:5-6

CHAPTER 7
PRACTICE MAKES CONFIDENCE

Paul told Timothy to 'stir up' the gift within him.[46] Again, the word gift is Greek *charisma,* favor one receives without merit of his own. To stir up is Greek *anazōpyreō,* and means to kindle up, inflame one's mind, strength, zeal. This is an awesome Greek word for it has three root words! They are *ana, zoon,* and *pyr.* It is a living being with a fire in the midst of them! Amazing!

The prophetic voice should be like a fire in the midst of us. If not, kindle it! Fire up!

I would like to introduce you to some practice exercises that can help stir up the prophetic voice within you.

Exercise One:
Listen to some news reports. Take notes of practice points. If there is a fire and officials are investigating whether or not it's arson, ask Holy Spirit if it is arson and write down what you believe you hear.

If there is a kidnapping or a missing person, ask Holy Spirit what happened and where the victim is at the moment. Are they dead or alive? Write down what you hear Holy Spirit say.

Anything you are inspired to ask about, write down the answer and then keep checking back with the news reports until they have their answer. Compare what is on your list to the findings. You will build a track record. At first you might be mostly wrong if you are

---

[46] 2 Timothy 1:6

new to receiving revelation by Holy Spirit. Eventually, you will sharpen your hearing and your accuracy will go up. However, perhaps you will have the actual answer and the officials involved in the news report will get it wrong. Just wait. They may get it right later. Sometimes reporters jump the gun and give false information. Just trust the process and develop a track record.

Early in my ministry my pastor's brother went missing. In a meeting with my pastor, he commented that I had not asked him about his brother. I said I knew he was alright because he just had to get away from all the voices of friends and family so he could think and make a decision. Sure enough, he showed up a few days later and that is exactly what he had done. This was when I understood I could practice receiving in this way.

Exercise Two:
This is one our prophetic itinerant group used to get ready for a series of meetings recently.

Ask someone to loan you pictures of living people they know but you do not know. It is best, but not required, if there is just one individual shown in each picture. Ask them not to tell you anything about the individuals in advance. Write down your immediate impressions from your Spirit. Then, without telling the person who provided the picture what you wrote, ask them about the individual and compare their answers to what you wrote.

I've only seen this method fail once and it wasn't really a failure. There were five of us practicing. There was one particular picture passed around for which none of us received anything by the Spirit. I asked to see the picture again. It came to me. I asked, "Is this person deceased?"

The person was, indeed, deceased so of course we didn't receive anything.

Exercise Three:
You have to be quick for this one.

If you are in a prophetic meeting with a prophet known for accuracy, have pen and paper ready and as fast as you can before they prophesy to someone, write your initial impressions. See how much they match what the minister says.

This is not a judge of whether you are right or wrong. The prophet of the meeting might just miss something, but it just gives you another source of possible confirmation of your ability to receive revelation.

Exercise Four:
Stop listening with just natural hearing.

Whenever someone is talking to you, listen in your Holy Spirit as well as in the natural. You will not only hear what they say, but will receive revelation about what they say. Then ask Holy Spirit what, if anything, you should do with this insight. If instructed to say or do something, step out in faith. In order to respect the individual I usually ask permission from them before I speak into their life or take any action. If they decline, hold your peace.

Exercise Five:
Don't jump out of bed too quickly.

During the seconds when you first wake up are prime moments of receiving downloads from God. I have trained myself to keep my eyes closed and just tune my spiritual hearing to Holy Spirit. In the shortest of time, I will receive huge downloads. At first I had to write them down because I could forget them later and sometimes I still do that if I know I have a busy day.

Of course this is easiest if you are waking up naturally and not by an alarm clock. Unless you have the luxury of setting your own schedule and don't require the alarm clock, this would require a decent bedtime so your body wakes without the clock.

I hope these exercises will be very useful to you as you grow in the prophetic ministry.

I sense I should share something else here. Prophecy can be so simple we almost dismiss it. It doesn't have to be some grand, elaborate statement. I was recently with a woman who, by her track record, is a reliable prophet.

I was asking her to be praying for me about the new direction of our ministry. She cut me off mid-sentence and said, "Just before you started talking to ask me that, I heard the word railway. That's all I heard, railway. Don't ask me what it means, but that's what I heard."

To the time of this writing, I don't know the significance of railway, but I know it's from God and I know at the right time I will find out what God means by 'railway'.

CHAPTER 8
HOLY SPIRIT AND YOUR LOCAL CHURCH

I am using the word 'church' in the traditional generic sense in this chapter. In fact, the born-again believers[1] are the church[2], exclusively, regardless of where they meet and in which religious denomination they gather. When the Bible speaks of the churches, it is most definitely intending to speak of the believers, not a building or denomination. I would prefer to say assembly, for example. Just know that for the purposes of this chapter, when I say church, I mean a local assembly or the body of Christ at large.

A gentlemen recently spoke with me about the services at his local church. He said, he often gets a prophetic word or an unction to speak in tongues during a service, but doesn't feel the freedom to do so.

I asked him if he had spoken to his pastor about this or were there any orientation classes offered that might explain the policy of that assembly. He didn't know about the classes for sure, but didn't think there were any. The church had gone through several pastors in recent years so there was a bit of confusion as to leadership policies. Also, the change in pastors made it difficult to get a handle on what the new pastor expected.

In addition, it was really an elder-run church rather than a pastor-led church. Perhaps I'll address this in a moment.

In general, among congregations there are five schools of

---

[1] Romans 10:9-10
[2] Matthew 18:17

thought on operating Holy Spirit in any form. They are:

1. Don't do it at all. No tongues, no prophecy, no nothing. Just say you are a Trinitarian and let Holy Spirit just dwell inside you and be quiet about it.
2. You can speak in tongues, but only the leader may interpret and you speak only by consent of leadership. Prophecy must be approved by an appointed leader before you can speak it out.
3. It's a free-for-all atmosphere. Anybody and everybody operates however they are inspired. We'll deal with the fall out later. Go for it!
4. We do it, but only during conferences or in one of the services that is NOT Sunday morning. We don't want to embarrass or drive away visitors with a display of God's power. We enjoy calling ourselves charismatic or Spirit filled, but we don't want to damage our reputation with anyone.
5. You can do it, but only after attending six weeks of classes and being released by leadership as a designated Holy Spirit operator. We'll give you a badge or special colored jacket so we know who you are.

You might think I am being tongue-in-cheek, but I have personally experienced all of these policies in churches across America.

The book of Acts and Paul's subsequent instructions concerning the manifestation of Holy Spirit in a corporate assembly ought to be enough to see a common policy within the Body of Christ, but you know how we are. We love our opinions.

If you join yourself to a local assembly, you are told in scripture to submit to authority. Therefore, find out first-hand what the policy of the church is BEFORE you become a member, if they have membership. If you don't agree with their policy or don't wish to abide by it, don't join. Perhaps you should just continue to attend services there, take classes and wait until the Lord tells you what to do. Maybe you will change your mind based on further instruction. Maybe you will discover you are in the wrong assembly. Maybe God will change things there.

At churches where I've pastored, we taught what was presented in Acts and Corinthians concerning operating Holy Spirit in an assembly. Then we exercised freedom, free flow of

Holy Spirit. If a problem arose, for example, a person operated in their flesh calling it Holy Spirit, we dealt with it in a loving professional way. Our policy was that we would rather have Holy Spirit operated freely in our midst than avoid the risk of embarrassment. We tried to provide an atmosphere in which people could feel comfortable practicing releasing their first prophetic words.

To be born-again is to be in the New Covenant relationship with the Godhead. The Godhead includes Holy Spirit. The word of God, beginning with the ministry of Jesus through Revelation, defines and describes New Covenant living. It is, I believe, irresponsible to pick out and throw out the power manifestation of Holy Spirit and reduce it to just some inward warm fuzzy.

Just a note about elder *run* (dictated) churches. . . In Ephesians 4, the Bible tells us of the function and offices of the ministry. The offices are Pastor, Apostle, Prophet, Teacher, and Evangelist. You will not see the office of Elder listed in the Ministry offices. Elders serve the church. Elders do not run the church. They can be part of the 'helps and government' God sets in the church, and therefore, their assignment should be chosen by God and not because of money, influence or other worldly considerations. They should meet the requirements of men and women of faith according to scriptures. (Yes, women can be elders).

They should be wise counsel to the pastor and they are mandated to pray and anoint the sick and other functions as described in the New Testament.

While elders are almost always well-intentioned, God-loving individuals, I believe elders have been allowed to overstep their boundaries and God-ordained function for the most part. In many cases they usurp the authority of the shepherd God placed in that assembly.

The work of an elder can be a beautiful thing and a great asset to the Body of Christ, but it can also be a playground for the Jezebel spirit.

CHAPTER 9
CONFIRMATION OR VAIN REPETITION?

When the Spirit of God is speaking to the church through prophets, it is not unusual to hear of or read several prophets giving the same word. This is called confirmation. God confirms God's word, with signs and wonders, but also with prophetic confirmations.

In Corinthians God even speaks about more than one prophet speaking in a meeting, but limits it to a few and the others judge.[1] Oops, there goes the theory of not judging anything. [2]

When we are new to flowing in the prophetic operation, we might fall into the trap of imitation. Imitation is not all bad. Even the apostle Paul said that the people should imitate him.[3] However, a prophetic word is fresh from Holy Spirit and should not sound like mimicking.

As a teacher, I have smiled to myself, when I hear students imitating their teacher. It is pretty easy to spot certain catch phrases or common words. By the way, it always leaves me a bit skeptical when I hear the prophet speaking on old King James English since that is not their native language. It almost seems like the prophecy is being presented by way of speaking in tongues which seems odd. Just talk normally and let Holy Spirit decide the language of the hearers.

---

[1] 1 Corinthians 14:29
[2] Matthew 7:1 (should be condemn not), 1 Corinthians 6:2
[3] 1 Corinthians 11:1

I recently did some research on prophetic words because it seemed to me that the prophets were repeating themselves more than just a confirming word. For example, January of that year was supposed to be a month of breakthrough. Then they said February was going to be the month of breakthrough. Wait for it. No, March was the month of breakthrough and so on and so on. Yes, they all could be a month of breakthrough, or is it vain repetition? Was it just so popular to use the word breakthrough? Were we all just so desperate for a break that our flesh was crying out and calling it prophecy?

Just because your pastor uses a certain phrase when prophesying does not dictate your use of that phrase. One church had a pastor that started every prophetic utterance with 'thus saith the Lord'. I know from experience that this is more of a 'get me started' comfort zone. The pastor had a good prophetic word, but just had to use that phrase to get himself started. Sure enough, everyone on the church began to use that phrase. Can you hear me laughing?

If what you hear in the Spirit to speak is unique, don't be afraid of it. You do not have to be saying what all the other prophets say in order for the word to be legit. If you do hear the same word as another prophet, that's not wrong. Just make sure you are getting a fresh word from Holy Spirit and not just repeating something because you are excited or pressured into prophesying and have to have something to say.

When prophets truly have a confirming word, there will be similarities, but I have found there will be a uniqueness among the similarities. Even in the Bible we see similarities among the prophecies of Isaiah and Jeremiah, for example. However, there is a uniqueness to each prophet.

Another pattern is a prophet who simply repeats what the Bible already says. It is encouraging and good because it is scripture, the good news of God, but is it prophecy? Prophecy will never ever contradict the word of God, but I don't need a prophet to tell me what the Bible already tells me. Prophecy is a fresh word from the Lord through Holy Spirit.

There is the pattern of 'just make 'em feel good.' That is, a prophet who tells you what you want to hear and not necessarily a fresh word from the Lord. I know of a couple of prophets who will always say the same things no matter how many times you hear them. It goes something like this: "You are the head and not the tail. You are highly favored of God. Breakthrough is about to happen. What you prayed, God heard and it is about to happen."

Can we say 'duh" boys and girls? These are all true for all believers. There is a false concept that unless prophecy is a feel good word, it is not true prophecy. That is not Biblical. Just read the prophecy of Jeremiah 23 and you find out that it was not a feel good word for the pastors who scattered the flock.

The word Jonah had for Nineveh was not a feel good word.[4]

No prophet should be a prophet in order to be famous. There are some prophets who have notoriety. That happens with a track record of accuracy. They get a following and get known. Most of the prophets are relatively unknown. They serve quietly, in obscurity, but they serve. Therefore, you will sometimes get such an awesome word from the Lord that excites you and where you are, the people will like it, but then one of the 'famous' prophets says the same thing a week later and the whole world is jumping on it. You think to yourself, "I just said that! I heard it first!'

Always know, God gets the glory. The prophet, famous or not, does not get the glory. God knows you heard God. God knows you obeyed and spoke what Holy Spirit delivered. That is enough.

My frustration has come because a prophetic word from an unknown prophet should carry the same weight of importance as the same word from a known prophet. I have heard prophetic words spoken in small local churches that were from God, no doubt. Later, when a famous prophet says the same thing, someone who I know was there when that same word was given in obscurity acts like they didn't hear it until the famous prophet spoke it. I have said, "Yes, _____ just spoke that word last week. Remember?"

Obviously, people are not honoring the prophetic word unless it comes from certain people. They follow the prophet rather than the prophetic word.

---

[4] Jonah 1:1

CHAPTER 10
THE NUTS AND BOLTS

I highly recommend you take my course, TNT, Taking New Territory.
The following information is taken from that course and presents the inspiration manifestations of Holy Spirit which are Tongues, Interpretation of Tongues and Prophecy.
You should also carefully read 1 Corinthians, chapters 12 and 14 as this study covers those chapters.

Tongues, Interpretation of Tongues and Prophecy

These three manifestations are closely related in function. They are sometimes called inspirational manifestations because they can be used to edify people. Paul was very clear about the proper usage of each manifestation in public gatherings.[1]

> 1 Corinthians 14:22-40 Wherefore tongues are for a sign, not to them that believe, but to them that believe not: but prophesying serves not for them that believe not, but for them which believe.

Tongues - are the language of Holy Spirit. They can be heard by

---

[1] 1 Corinthians 14:22-40

those listening as though it were their own language, or they will remain unknown until there is an interpretation. Even if you speak in tongues in a certain way one time, they might sound completely different the next time. You do not think of what you will say. It comes from Holy Spirit as you yield to God. Tongues has a both a public purpose and a private purpose.

> Jude 20 But ye, beloved, building up yourselves on your most holy faith, praying in (by or through) the Holy Ghost (Spirit),

The words 'praying in the Holy Ghost (Spirit)' can be speaking to yourself in an unknown tongue. It can also be praying in your own language, but as led by Holy Spirit and not your own thoughts. We should do both. There have been times I have been inspired to pray for someone I have never met or for a situation for which I have no knowledge. But, most of the time, I just speak in tongues privately. Both ways build me up and make me stronger in the faith.

> Acts 19:6 And when Paul had laid his hands upon them, the Holy Ghost came on them; and they spoke with tongues, and prophesied.

Biblical evidence shows that once a believer has Holy Spirit, that believer can operate any and all of the manifestations. Many man-made doctrines say a believer may only receive one or a few of the 'gifts' from God, meaning even if a person can prophesy, they might not ever speak in tongues. This is wrong. Holy Spirit is activated in the believer by obedience and the purpose of God. Paul even said the "Spirit of the prophets is subject to the prophets". Paul spoke in tongues often.[2]

Interpretation of Tongues - is not a translation of what was spoken in the unknown tongue, but gives the idea or thought of what Holy Spirit was saying in the tongues. It comes by Holy Spirit and NOT by our own understanding.[3]

Tongues is a sign to people who don't believe. Compare this to

---

[2] Acts 10:46a, 1 Corinthians 14:18
[3] 1 Corinthians 14:22

prophecy which is for those who believe.

This difference has really been missed or misunderstood in the church. Many churches avoid speaking in tongues with interpretation in the presence of new visitors who are pre-converts, but those are exactly the people God intended tongues for a sign!

While for our own edification, we can speak in tongues any time, God gave a few criteria for corporate use in an assembly.[4] God limited the participants to two or three, but no more (at the most). God insisted there be interpretation in this case.

In public use, tongues needs to be interpreted in order for people to know what God is saying. Also, when you are speaking in tongues privately in your prayer time, you may interpret as well, if you desire to or you may just speak in tongues. Publicly tongues MUST be interpreted. The interpretation can be operated by the one who speaks in tongues or by another person. Please note that many Christian-based denominations have opinions differing from what scripture says about the operation of Holy Spirit. In this course, we are sticking to what God's word tells us, that there must be interpretation.

Prophecy - is foretelling. It involves the future. It is NOT fortune telling or prediction! It is the decree of God about what will happen, sometimes with conditions (i.e. "If you do this, such and such will happen")

God intends for us to welcome the prophetic word, unrestricted by gender or status.[5]

Prophecy is definitely for the end times or now. The prophetic words have a specific purpose as seen in both

In the Old Testament, false prophets were put to death, but now we are in the time of grace and God will take care of dealing with false prophets. If we know the Word of God, and are sensitive to Holy Spirit, we will not be fooled by false prophecies. Prophetic words will NEVER disagree with the written Word of God.

1 Corinthians 14:29-32 gives specific instructions for corporate use of prophetic words. The prophetic word is to come through two or three prophets and the others judge. The Greek word for judge is *diakrino* and means to prefer or withdraw. This is a position of respect. It is other prophets saying in essence, 'I

---

[4] 1 Corinthians 14:27-28
[5] 1 Thessalonians 5:20, Acts 21:9, Acts 2:18

respect your ability to flow in Holy Spirit by prophecy and recognize the accuracy.'

This instruction is so missed in teaching the operation of the prophetic in public service. I have ministered with people who don't know this truth and respect. They, in their zealousness, walk all over the prophetic word of other prophets and usually are inaccurate in their manifestation because they are out of order. I usually have to ask them not to 'piggyback' me in ministry.

I once requested of a fellow minister that they not interfere with the prophetic word Holy Spirit had just instructed me to give. What I meant was, when God does a work through one prophet, let that work without adding on something. (I know sometimes multiple person ministry is appropriate, but in this case the additional words were causing confusion and therefore not of God. The minister informed me that if God gave them something, they were going to give it out. That almost sounds bold, but in fact, 1 Corinthians 14:20-32 is teaching just the opposite.

Avoiding this scenario should not cause us to stop operating spiritual matters, but it should cause us to ask God concerning what we are receiving.

There is an additional instruction that while people are learning to prophesy they all may speak for the sake of learning.[6] The spirits of the prophets are subject to the prophets. To be subject means to be put in order. Prophets are expected to know and observe the boundaries and freedoms God has placed around the prophetic operation.

Although in public use, the prophetic word comes from two or three prophets, (for a corporate prophetic word to the group), personal prophetic words, even in a group setting can be spoken to individuals without limit. I often receive prophetic words for each and every individual in meetings where I preach and teach.

It is important that I stress again, if you are attending or ministering in a church where they have a different understanding of scripture or a policy concerning operation of Holy Spirit that is contrary to the way I am showing you in this book, you must respect authority. God does not want confusion or division or strife among the Body of Christ.

Tradition has dictated tongues is the starting point to operate everything else. This is not necessarily the case. I have found that many people come to salvation already sensitive to things of the

---

[6] 1 Corinthians 14:31

spirit realm. They may call it intuition, sixth sense or something else, but it is most definitely a spiritual sensitivity.

They easily make the transition to Word of Knowledge and Word of Wisdom, but may struggle at tongues and interpretation. They may also be uncomfortable with prophecy because of previous exposure to psychics. The apparent similarity (at least to their unlearned ears) may be a barrier for a time.

When we get it through our head that it is by the Spirit and not by might,[7] then we might breakthrough to the freedom God gives us. We will know we can fully operate Holy Spirit in all its manifestations to the glory and purpose of God.

Considering the fruit of the Spirit, if you can operate love, you can operate gentleness, for example because they are all fruit of the Spirit. In the same manner, if you can speak in tongues, you can operate the other eight manifestations listed in 1 Corinthians. Or, if you just operate Word of Wisdom, you can operate the other eight because they are all by the Spirit, not by your might or power.

No matter where you are in this equation, desire more. Desire to operate all fruit of Holy Spirit and all manifestations of Holy Spirit. If you are already operating all of these, desire to operate more and more effectively, more accurately. Stir up the gift within you. Sharpen your skill.[8]

---

[7] Zechariah 4:6
[8] Hebrews 5:14

CHAPTER 11
CONTINUOUS PROCESS IMPROVEMENT

Continuous Process Improvement is a catch phrase I picked up from the corporate world. I believe it is self-explanatory, however, let me elaborate.

Although we always want to stick to Biblical absolutes, there are many things about God that are always changing. God used a burning bush once for a sign as far as we know, but did not repeat that process. Yes, Jonah was swallowed by a fish, but I can't recall God doing that one again.

You and I are never at a point where we are finished learning from God. Today, you might be a fantastic accurate prophet and God speaks through you in a certain way. Don't get too comfortable in the status quo. Apply continuous process improvement and allow God free course to change the way you do things. What served well yesterday might not be what God wants to do today. Jesus spit in clay and rubbed it on a man's eyes. That worked then, but the next time Jesus did things another way.

Also, we are humans communicating to humans. I can always perfect my delivery. I can learn to speak more clearly, to move around a room full of people more efficiently, improve and increase my vocabulary. In short, I as a human, need to make sure nothing about me gets in the way of what God is doing.

While a layman might not be skilled in the use of a microphone, a keynote speaker absolutely should be. If you are in ministry of any kind, learn how to use a microphone properly.

One minister, who will remain nameless was watching a video of themselves ministering in a gathering. They were appalled to see they had been chomping on gum the whole time! Not until they saw the video did they realize this. While it is not a crime to chew gum (in most countries), it was not attractive and in some cultures would be offensive.

Another minister had neglected to wear a slip under her skirt and when she was up on the raised platform with stage lights everyone could see through the material. Fortunately an assistant pulled her off stage and gave her the slip she was wearing.

Would God be hindered by either of these scenarios? NO! But the people to whom they were speaking might be distracted by these things. We can't please everyone or avoid all potential offenses, but we can improve ourselves along the way.

Most speakers have nervous habits that will disappear over time. Mine was continually asking, "You know?" It was very irritating to the hearers when repeated frequently throughout the message.

Some groups like a more energetic approach while others call for a softer delivery. All this can be discerned through Holy Spirit.

Some venues can accommodate longer ministry time while others require a strict schedule. With practice and polite sensitivity, the speaker can work within these parameters.

In general, the person bringing the prophetic word will not be a minister presenting the whole meeting, but will be a lady here, a gentleman there. They are not keynote speakers, they are not the pastor, they are not a Sunday School teacher, but are simply children of God who hear God's voice telling them to speak. They obey.

Even these individuals can have continuous process improvement. Their nervous stuttering and hesitation will diminish. Their delivery will become more eloquent with experience. They will gain confidence over time.

The first way you can improve your process is to open your mouth and begin to utter the mysteries God is saying through you! Be available to God. Be obedient to God. Prophesy with a foundation of love for the people and respect for the Church.

You may or may not function as a Prophet, but you most definitely are prophetic if you are born again.

Now, GO. . . STAND . . . AND SPEAK!

Go, stand and speak in the temple to the people
all the words of this life. Acts 5:20

ABOUT THE AUTHOR

Dr. Linda Smith – Christian, pastor, teacher, author, and minister. She is the founder of Free Them Ministries, Inc., an international Christian outreach, and pastored PowerHouse Christian Center in San Marcos, Texas.

With a Ph.D. in Theology, and a gift for teaching, Linda presents the dynamic word of God in a way that personalizes the message for the hearer. Students come away from Dr. Smith's classes with an excitement for the word of God and an ability to find out for themselves the meaning of the scriptures. Dr. Smith has served the church for over thirty years educating people of all ages with the Word of God. She has also served on the faculty board of Christian universities and was the Christian Education Director in several churches across America.

Linda uses the Bible, humor and her testimony to exhort the people of God seek a more intimate walk with the Lord Jesus Christ. Her ministry is a mandate to create spiritual maturity and integrity in churches, businesses and homes and she does so with anointed messages that glorify God. This minister of God is Holy Spirit filled and has a sincere desire in her heart for the Bride of Christ to be fully prepared for marriage to the Bridegroom.

To schedule this dynamic speaker, contact Free Them Ministries, Inc., P. O. Box 708, San Marcos, TX 78667

www.ingramcontent.com/pod-product-compliance
Lightning Source LLC
LaVergne TN
LVHW051806080426
835511LV00019B/3424